KANGA, MY DRAGON OF ANGER

A book about Anger

Written and Illustrated

By Doctor Harmony

ACKNOWLEDGEMENTS

I would like to thank my mother, husband and children for their love, patience and support. Without them, my books would not have been possible.

I also wish to thank my friends and other family members for their invaluable opinions, advice and assistance in producing this book series.

Last but not least, I wish to thank all the patients who I have worked with in their recovery process. They have inspired me to write the Building Resilience series.

Building Resilience Series
Series Number One
"Kanga, My Dragon of Anger" Copyright 2015
Australia
Written and Illustrated by Doctor Harmony

National Library of Australia
Cataloguing-in-Publication data:
Doctor Harmony
Kanga, My Dragon of Anger.

ISBN 978-1-925420-00-5

Printed in USA

www.doctorharmony.com

Meet my pet dragon, Kanga, who lives in my pocket.
He sticks out his head when I'm as angry as a rocket.

Kanga breathes fire into my head and belly.
Staying calm when I'm angry, happens rarely.
When I'm cranky, my thoughts race
And my heart beats at a fast pace.

When I am angry I stomp, I clomp, I scream, I shout,
Whenever people aren't listening to what I'm talking about.

Kanga awakes and makes
me roar
If my little brother takes my
lolly store.

When Mum and Dad say, "No"
To that party, where I want to go.

Kanga blows out fire when I keep making the same mistake,
While doing my homework, it feels I'm sinking in a lake,
Not getting anywhere with all that hard work.
Irritation, frustration and anger will lurk.

When my sister cheats during the game
After our points started off being the same,
Kanga roars, "It's not fair!"
So I explode without any care,
Not being aware that people may get hurt
By my actions which can be rude and curt.

My parents then scream
That we are no longer a team.
My sister then cries,
With tears pouring from her eyes.

Kanga, the dragon, has done it again!
He makes me forget to count to ten,
When I feel angry and should give my mind a rest.
Staying calm seems to be the hardest test.

I decide to give it one more try.
To keep my beloved sister's face dry
Because I really don't like seeing her cry.
I forget what it's like for those close by
When I explode, and feel my brain will fry.

I say sorry to my family.
I apologise to my sister, Emily.
I tell them that if I'm angry, I will
walk away
Until I am calm, and will talk to
them later that day.

**I make a promise that when I'm away, I will count to ten
And breathe slowly while repeating the word "Zen".**

I will go back and talk about what annoyed me.
Sometimes it's because of something I didn't see.
It may be that they saw it a different way.
Once it's all sorted, I'm happy and go away to play.

These days Kanga mostly hides back in my pocket
Because with the new me, I rarely go off my rocket.

KIDS PAGES

It is normal to feel angry. It is what you do with the anger that is important. If you scream, stomp, throw things, hurt people or slam doors and remain angry, it hurts other people and it does not feel good.

Can you complete the drawing of Al when he is angry?

Can you remember when you were last angry? Draw what your dragon of anger looks like.

What does your dragon get angry about? Can you draw different times when your dragon comes out of your pocket and is angry?

What can you do that will help the situation when you feel angry?

Find the following answers amongst the letters. Look across, down and diagonally:

SLOW BREATHS   FEEL FOR OTHERS
WALK AWAY   CALM DOWN
COUNT TO TEN   ACCEPT THE SITUATION
TALK CALMLY   LAUGH AT IT
BE KIND   CHECK WITH OTHERS

A	C	C	E	P	T	T	H	E	S	I	T	U	A	T	I	O	N
Z	O	H	F	S	E	U	N	T	O	P	F	Y	U	A	D	F	G
X	U	W	E	R	L	K	E	A	E	U	T	P	I	L	W	Y	L
E	N	J	E	C	A	L	M	D	O	W	N	C	E	K	H	K	I
W	T	L	L	A	K	Y	Z	P	I	T	F	H	U	C	S	R	E
Q	T	I	F	G	L	W	D	A	I	O	B	M	E	A	W	R	S
I	O	S	O	U	Y	C	I	O	F	D	M	E	B	L	A	M	H
R	T	N	R	S	C	F	M	T	R	E	A	Z	R	M	B	I	O
S	E	M	O	A	S	Y	W	T	H	I	N	B	L	L	Q	U	E
W	N	E	T	E	V	W	O	P	A	O	B	E	A	Y	M	E	Y
U	K	W	H	O	L	A	U	G	H	A	T	I	T	E	A	L	P
P	T	J	E	T	U	L	P	A	O	N	M	H	S	R	Y	H	P
H	U	B	R	E	A	K	S	Y	P	E	N	B	E	K	I	N	D
E	L	I	S	K	Q	A	W	E	T	M	G	E	A	R	Y	P	E
N	R	O	C	Q	A	W	N	E	Y	K	F	L	U	T	S	W	A
Y	Y	P	U	R	C	A	H	G	D	A	O	V	U	Z	S	A	I
S	P	D	O	L	B	Y	S	V	U	J	U	Y	E	P	N	A	S
A	I	N	S	L	O	W	B	R	E	A	T	H	S	M	A	H	D

It is also important to ask what you have learnt from this situation or if there is anything you could have done differently. If you blame other people for the situation, you are more likely to get angry because you will think things have not been fair.

Help AI to calm down as he takes slow breaths.

Join the dots.

Help angry Al calm down and find his way to talk about things.

START

END

To simplify the steps, when you are angry remember:
1) Leave
2) Breathe
3) Speak

Talk to trusted adults if you need to talk this through.

If you ever need extra help, you may like to talk to a counsellor, your local doctor, psychologist or your school counsellor.

Remember that there is always help available.

PARENTS PAGE

Dealing with our own anger and the anger of others is one of the biggest challenges for many people. We may not be aware that we are angry and may react thoughtlessly instead.

It is important to be aware of our feelings as early as possible and to own the feeling rather than blaming other people or the situation. The more we think that an injustice has been done towards us, the more indignant and angry we will feel. It also means we have given others control over our feelings and behaviour, which makes us feel more helpless.

If we are too angry to think clearly and talk calmly, it is best to walk away, take slow breaths and count to ten or do a relaxing activity. When we are calmer, it is easier to reflect on why we got angry. It may be helpful to ask ourselves:

- Did I contribute to the situation?
- Is it possible that I misunderstood the situation?
- Are there other reasons for what happened?
- Did I hurt anyone? What can I do to make amends?

Once we have calmed down and reflected, return to those involved to discuss it as calmly as possible, without blaming. Start with: "I felt ... because ..." Check with them on how they saw the situation.

To simplify the steps for children:

1) Leave
2) Breathe
3) Speak

It may be helpful to ask your children:

- What do you do when your Kanga gets angry?
- What happens afterwards? How do other people react?
- How do other people behave when they are angry? How do you react when they are angry?
- Can you think of any other ways you can deal with Kanga?

BUILDING RESILIENCE BOOK SERIES

"Kanga, My Dragon of Anger" is part of series one in the Building Resilience range of books.

The author, Dr Harmony is an Australian psychiatrist and mother who is dedicated to building a more resilient and confident young generation. The books are based on her clinical practice as a psychiatrist and her personal experience.

She has seen many adults in clinical practice, for over fourteen years, with issues related to low self-confidence and self-esteem and difficulties coping with uncomfortable feelings, Dr Harmony is passionate about addressing these issues in childhood, with the hope of preventing mental illness in later life.

Dr Harmony hopes to encourage children to identify their feelings, to express in constructive ways and to take positive action. By openly discussing the topics in a non-threatening and fun way, it helps children realise that other kids have similar experiences, that they are not alone and there is nothing to be embarrassed about.

The books aim to help children to be aware of feelings, to talk about them, and to have courage to deal with challenges they may encounter.

The series give children, teachers and parents advice on how to deal with common situations and uncomfortable feelings. It also encourages parent-child discussion about difficult topics.

Some topics (even common life events such as death) are traditionally taboo or are challenging for adults to talk about. If adults are uncomfortable talking about issues, it is even more difficult for children to discuss them or to know how to effectively cope with situations. Even feelings can be difficult to discuss for some adults. This range of books opens the communication pathways and helps children and adults to face matters without shame, embarrassment or stigma.

The books are designed to be thought-provoking and entertaining. They are aimed at 5 to 12 year old children but even adults may find them beneficial.

Each book has hidden characters in the pictures and educational activities, which add an extra dimension of fun.

To make the most of the books, it is suggested that parents discuss the book contents with the child. Thereafter, it is suggested that you refer to the characters, feelings and situations in daily life as they arise. For instance, if your child is visibly angry and distressed or agitated, refer to "Kanga, the angry dragon". Discuss the feelings and ask, "What can we do to put Kanga back in your pocket?" When your child is calm, discuss what made him/her angry (see Parents page).

CPSIA information can be obtained at www.ICGtesting.com
Printed in the USA
LVIW01n1508220816
501363LV00015B/103